DENVER BRONCOS · SUPER BOWL CHAMPIONS

XXXII, JANUARY 25, 1998

31-24 VERSUS GREEN BAY PACKERS

XXXIII, JANUARY 31, 1999

34-19 VERSUS ATLANTA FALCONS

SUPER BOWL CHAMPIONS

DENVER BRONCOS

AARON FRISCH

CREATIVE EDUCATION

COVER: TIGHT END SHANNON SHARPE

PAGE 2: QUARTERBACK JOHN ELWAY LOOKING FOR A RECEIVER

RIGHT: WIDE RECEIVER BRANDON MARSHALL MAKING A CATCH

Published by Creative Education
P.O. Box 227, Mankato, Minnesota 56002
Creative Education is an imprint of The Creative Company
www.thecreativecompany.us

Book and cover design by Blue Design (www.bluedes.com)
Art direction by Rita Marshall
Printed by Corporate Graphics in the United States of America

Photographs by Dreamstime (Rosco), Getty Images (James Balog, Harry Benson, Andrew D. Bernstein, Steve Dykes, George Gojkovich, Rod Hanna/NFL, Andy Lyons, Al Messerschmidt/NFL, Doug Pensinger, Doug Pensinger/Allsport, Jamie Squire, Greg Trott, Ron Vesely, Dilip Vishwanat, Lou Witt/NFL)

Library of Congress Cataloging-in-Publication Data

Frisch, Aaron.
Denver Broncos / by Aaron Frisch.
p. cm. — (Super Bowl champions)
Includes index.
Summary: An elementary look at the Denver Broncos professional football team, including its formation in 1960, most memorable players, Super Bowl championships, and stars of today.
ISBN 978-1-60818-017-2
1. Denver Broncos (Football team)—History—Juvenile literature. I. Title. II. Series.

GV956.D4F748 2011
796.332'64'0978883—dc22   2009053502

CPSIA: 040110 PO1141

First Edition
9 8 7 6 5 4 3 2 1

CONTENTS

SUPER BOWL CHAMPIONS

Denver is a city in Colorado. It is nicknamed the "Mile-High City" because it is in the Rocky Mountains. Denver has a **stadium** called Invesco Field that is the home of a football team called the Broncos.

BRONCOS FACTS

First season:
1960

Conference/division:
American Football Conference, West Division

Super Bowl championships:
XXXII, January 25, 1998
31-24 versus Green Bay Packers

XXXIII, January 31, 1999
34-19 versus Atlanta Falcons

Training camp location:
Englewood, Colorado

NFL Web site for kids:
http://nflrush.com

The Broncos are part of the National Football League (NFL). All the teams in the NFL try to win the Super Bowl to become world champions. The Broncos' uniforms are **navy** and orange. One of their main **rivals** is the Kansas City Chiefs.

SUPER BOWL CHAMPIONS

The Broncos played their first season in 1960. They were part of a different **league** called the American Football League then. They had some good players like wide receiver Al Denson. But they lost a lot of games.

SUPER BOWL CHAMPIONS

In the 1970s, the Broncos played such tough defense that fans called them the "Orange Crush." Fans filled the Broncos' stadium for every game. The Broncos played in Super Bowl XII (12) after the 1977 season, but they lost.

In 1980, Denver hired a coach named Dan Reeves. In 1983, the Broncos got a new quarterback named John Elway. He led his team to the **playoffs** many times.

In 1998, Elway helped Denver win Super Bowl XXXII (32). The Broncos won Super Bowl XXXIII (33) the next year, too! Denver added fast cornerback Champ Bailey after that, but it could not win any more Super Bowls.

... CHAMP BAILEY HELPED DENVER BY MAKING MANY INTERCEPTIONS ...

... FLOYD LITTLE (LEFT) AND TOM JACKSON (RIGHT) ...

Two of the Broncos' first stars were Floyd Little and Tom Jackson. Little was a quick running back who played in Denver for nine seasons. Jackson was a smart linebacker.

WHY ARE THEY CALLED THE BRONCOS?

Colorado has a lot of rodeos. In a rodeo, cowboys ride wild horses called "broncos" that try to buck them off. In the 1920s, Denver also had a baseball team called the Broncos.

Denver added tight end Shannon Sharpe in 1990. He caught more passes in his career than any other tight end in NFL history. Running back Terrell Davis was another Broncos star. He scored 23 touchdowns in 1998.

SUPER BOWL CHAMPIONS

The Broncos added defensive end Elvis Dumervil in 2006. He was good at chasing down quarterbacks. Denver fans hoped that he would help lead the Broncos to their third Super Bowl championship!

... TEAMS HAD A HARD TIME TRYING TO BLOCK ELVIS DUMERVIL ...

SUPER BOWL CHAMPIONS

GLOSSARY

career — all the seasons that a person plays

league — a group of teams that all play against each other

navy — a color that is very dark blue

playoffs — games that the best teams play after a season to see who the champion will be

rivals — teams that play extra hard against each other

stadium — a large building that has a sports field and many seats for fans

INDEX